The Thinking Tree

CREATIVE WRITING PROMPTS AND VOCABULARY BUILDING

WRITING TIME WORKBOOK

Fun-Schooling With

MINECRAFT

Number Games and Comics

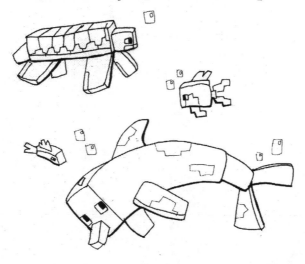

The Thinking Tree, LLC
FUNSCHOOLING.COM

NAME

_____

Date: _____

Age: _____

CREATED BY
Sarah Janisse Brown

ARTWORK BY
Susannah Brown age 13
Math Games by Alexandra Bretush

CREATIVE WRITING PROMPTS BY

Matty Sunny Light age 12
Amelie Moon Light age 14
Lily Star Light age 7
Joseph Brown age 10
Joshua Miller
Arti Mahendra Sharma
Kirsten Crawford Turner

EDITING AND IDEAS BY
Sue Gerdes
Hannah Corey

INSTRUCTIONS:
Follow the prompts on each page
to create a portfolio of your
creative writing experience.

Supplies:
Dictionary
Writing & Drawing Tools

Finish the Story

You are in the End city and a shulker shoots a bullet at you. You are floating higher and higher until you suddenly stop floating and begin falling...

Complete the Comic

Base your comic on the story you just wrote.

TITLE:_____

Write Your Own Story

Base your story on the illustration.

Add an illustration.

Write a Creative Story Using this Word List

Use math to finish the picture and find out what your story should be about.

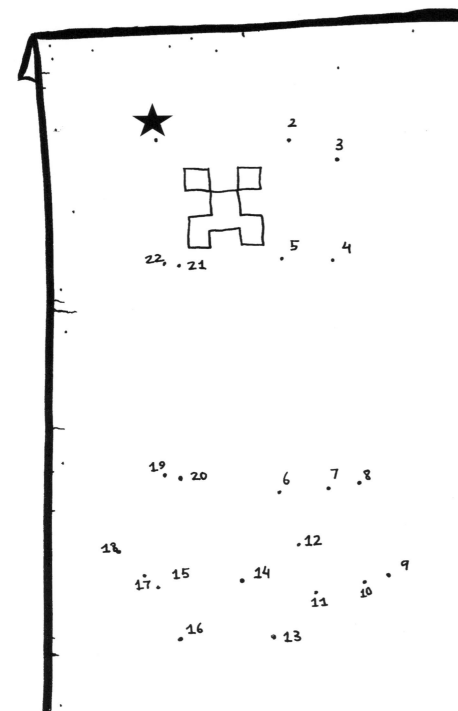

NOUNS:
bedrock
bucket
chicken
diamond
friend

ADJECTIVES:
fancy
golden
light
miniature
mossy
tropical

VERBS:
attack
build

Start with the star and connect the dots, counting by **ONES**.

Vocabulary Building:

Define three words that are not familiar to you:

1._____

2._____

3._____

Finish the Story

He held his breath as he stepped through the portal and into the Netherworld. The heat was unbearable, but necessary to face, for this was the only place to find the rare resources needed to survive. Suddenly, he

Complete the Comic

Base your comic on the story you just wrote.

TITLE:_____

Write Your Own Story

Base your story on the illustration.

Add an illustration.

Write a Creative Story Using this Word List

Use math to finish the picture and find out what your story should be about.

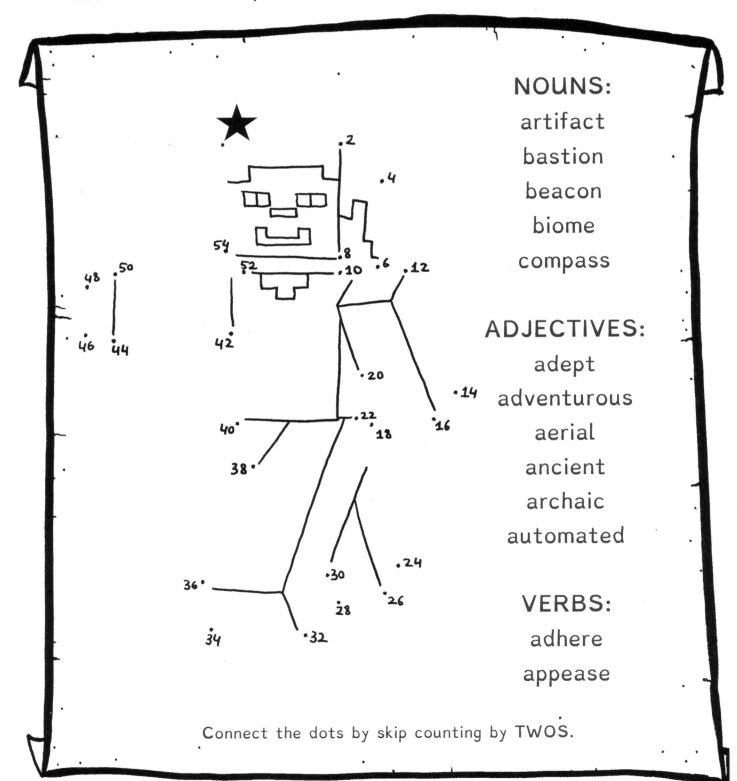

NOUNS:
artifact
bastion
beacon
biome
compass

ADJECTIVES:
adept
adventurous
aerial
ancient
archaic
automated

VERBS:
adhere
appease

Connect the dots by skip counting by TWOS.

Vocabulary Building:

Define three words that are not familiar to you:

1. _____

2. _____

3. _____

Finish the Story

You are being attacked by a wither. You have an army of zombies with full diamond gear to protect you. Just when you think you have the situation under control the Ender dragon appears in the

Complete the Comic

Base your comic on the story you just wrote.

TITLE:_____

Write Your Own Story

Base your story on the illustration.

_____

_____

_____

_____

_____

_____

_____

_____

_____

_____

Add an illustration.

Write a Creative Story Using this Word List

Use math to finish the picture and find out what your story should be about.

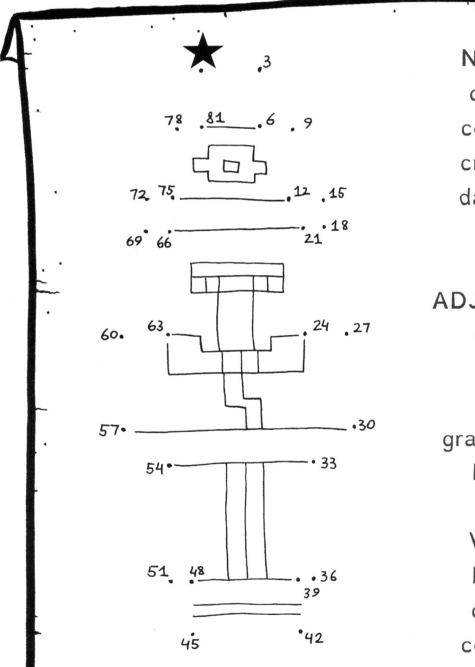

NOUNS:
conduit
conquest
crossbow
dandelion
debris

ADJECTIVES:
clumsy
daring
fragile
gravitational
harmful

VERBS:
butcher
conquer
construct

Connect the dots by skip counting by THREES.

Vocabulary Building:

Define three words that are not familiar to you:

1. _____

2. _____

3. _____

Finish the Story

I am in a woodland mansion trying to get the totem of undying. I'm fighting the Evoker and am surrounded by Vexes. Just as I am about to...

Complete the Comic

Base your comic on the story you just wrote.

TITLE:_____

Write Your Own Story

Base your story on the illustration.

Add an illustration.

Write a Creative Story Using this Word List

Use math to finish the picture and find out what your story should be about.

NOUNS:
dragon egg
dynamite
elytra
emerald
eternity

ADJECTIVES:
nomadic
scarce
terrifying
towering
vast

VERBS:
detonate
disappear
enhance

4

100   96   .12   .8
88   92   .20
16
76   32

56 52 40
72 68   36

84 .80   .28

64 60 48 .44

Connect the dots by skip counting by FOURS.

Vocabulary Building:

Define three words that are not familiar to you:

1. _____

2. _____

3. _____

Finish the Story

You are in a lightning storm and you see a zombie coming at you. You only have one weapon...

_____
_____
_____
_____
_____
_____
_____
_____
_____
_____
_____
_____
_____
_____
_____
_____
_____
_____
_____

Complete the Comic

Base your comic on the story you just wrote.

TITLE:_____

Write Your Own Story

Base your story on the illustration.

_____

_____

_____

_____

_____

_____

_____

_____

_____

_____

Add an illustration.

Write a Creative Story Using this Word List

Use math to finish the picture and find out what your story should be about.

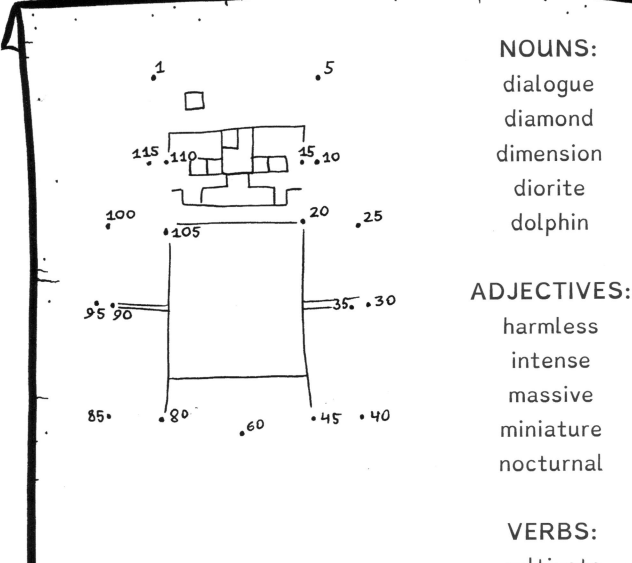

NOUNS:
dialogue
diamond
dimension
diorite
dolphin

ADJECTIVES:
harmless
intense
massive
miniature
nocturnal

VERBS:
cultivate
damage
dedicate

Connect the dots by skip counting by FIVES.

Vocabulary Building:

Define three words that are not familiar to you:

1. _____

2. _____

3. _____

Finish the Story

You are mining in a cave. You have dynamite and a pickaxe. You are searching for spawners and hear a crashing sound in the distance...

Complete the Comic

Base your comic on the story you just wrote.

TITLE:_____

Write Your Own Story

Base your story on the illustration.

Add an illustration.

Write a Creative Story Using this Word List

Use math to finish the picture and find out what your story should be about.

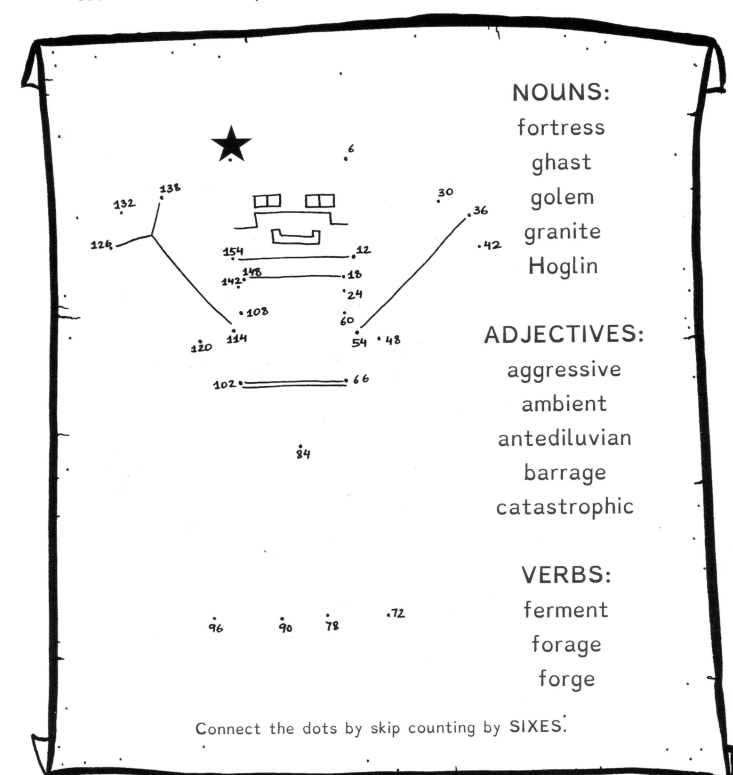

NOUNS:
fortress
ghast
golem
granite
Hoglin

ADJECTIVES:
aggressive
ambient
antediluvian
barrage
catastrophic

VERBS:
ferment
forage
forge

Connect the dots by skip counting by SIXES.

Vocabulary Building:

Define three words that are not familiar to you:

1. _____

_____

2. _____

_____

3. _____

_____

Finish the Story

You are being attacked by three withers and an army of wither skeletons. You must do everything in your power to protect the Ender Dragon egg

Complete the Comic

Base your comic on the story you just wrote.

TITLE:_____

Write Your Own Story

Base your story on the illustration.

Add an illustration.

Write a Creative Story Using this Word List

Use math to finish the picture and find out what your story should be about.

NOUNS:
honeycomb
librarian
lightening
membrane

nether star
ADJECTIVES:
cavernous
crimson
dearth

dilatory
dormant
VERBS:
rebirth
receive

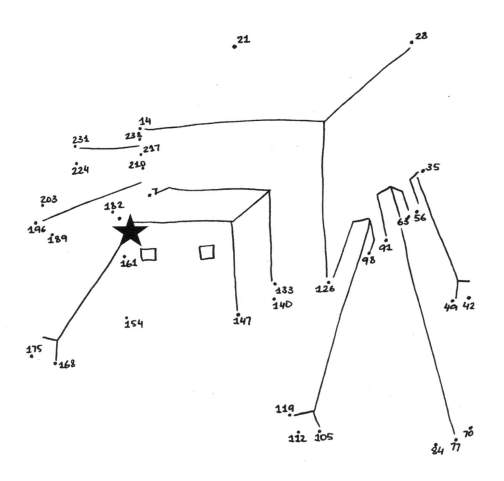

Connect the dots by skip counting by SEVENS.

Vocabulary Building:

Define three words that are not familiar to you:

1. _____

2. _____

3. _____

Finish the Story

His boat approaches the shore and he looks around, wondering what he can create on this uncharted territory. He imagines a large mansion or a humble farm with sheep and...

_____
_____
_____
_____
_____
_____
_____
_____
_____
_____
_____
_____
_____
_____
_____
_____
_____
_____
_____
_____

Complete the Comic

Base your comic on the story you just wrote.

TITLE:_____

Write Your Own Story

Base your story on the illustration.

Add an illustration.

Write a Creative Story Using this Word List

Use math to finish the picture and find out what your story should be about.

NOUNS:
novice
observer
parrot
Piglin

pillager
ADJECTIVES:
enigmatic
exorbitant
flammable

fortuitous
galactic
VERBS:
spawn
teleport

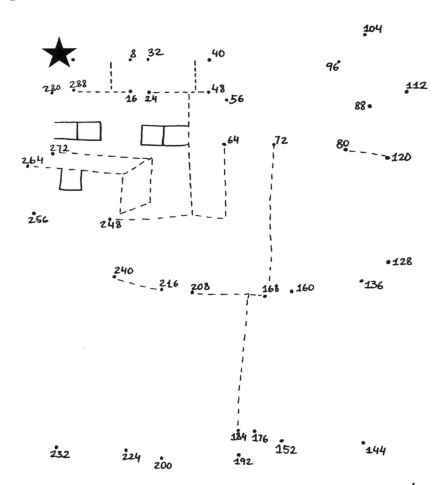

Connect the dots by skip counting by EIGTHS.

Vocabulary Building:

Define three words that are not familiar to you:

1. _____

2. _____

3. _____

Finish the Story

He entered the mine, not thinking to look behind him. He had his trusty pickaxe and was ready to dig in. Suddenly, he heard rattling bones and an arrow flew past him...

_____
_____
_____
_____
_____
_____
_____
_____
_____
_____
_____
_____
_____
_____
_____
_____
_____
_____

Complete the Comic

Base your comic on the story you just wrote.

TITLE:_____

Write Your Own Story

Base your story on the illustration.

Add an illustration.

Write a Creative Story Using this Word List

Use math to finish the picture and find out what your story should be about.

NOUNS:
potions
prologue
revenger
remnant

resources
ADJECTIVES:
lucrative
malleable
piercing

planetary
plethora
VERBS:
disseminate
elaborate

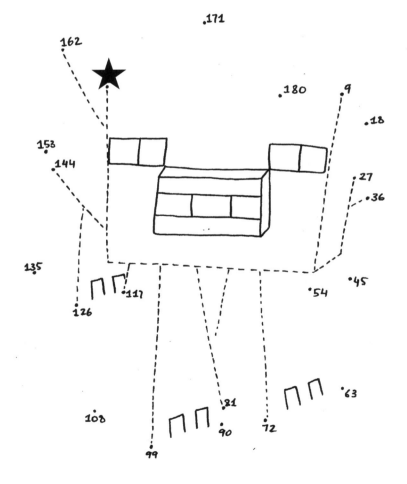

Connect the dots by skip counting by NINES.

_____
_____
_____
_____
_____
_____
_____
_____
_____
_____
_____
_____
_____
_____
_____
_____
_____
_____
_____
_____
_____
_____

Vocabulary Building:

Define three words that are not familiar to you:

1. _____

2. _____

3. _____

Finish the Story

I was busy mining for diamonds in a mossy cave when I saw some iron. I decided to craft a stone pickaxe to replace my wood tool. Suddenly, I noticed some light. Thinking it was another player, I moved towards it. I realized it was lava and I turned around to go back when a creeper and some zombies came running towards me. I

Complete the Comic

Base your comic on the story you just wrote.

TITLE:_____

Write Your Own Story

Base your story on the illustration.

Add an illustration.

Write a Creative Story Using this Word List

Use math to finish the picture and find out what your story should be about.

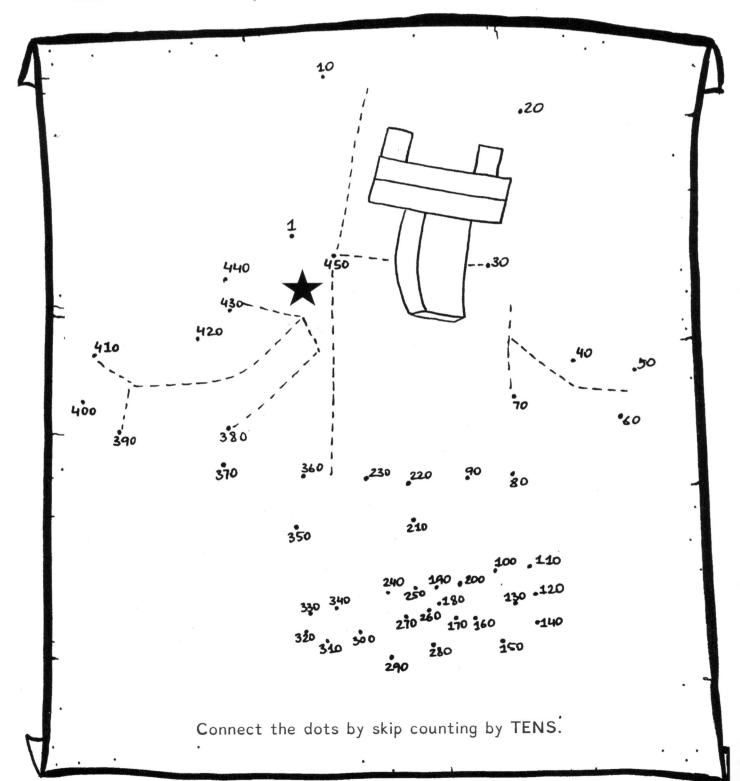

Connect the dots by skip counting by TENS.

NOUNS:
trident
sensor
ADJECTIVES:
skeleton
precarious
thunder
prestigious
treasure
prodigious

profuse
prolific
VERBS:
explore
pixelate

_____
_____
_____
_____
_____
_____
_____
_____
_____
_____
_____
_____
_____

Vocabulary Building:

Define three words that are not familiar to you:

1._____

_____

2._____

_____

3._____

_____

Finish the Story

Entity 303 is the most extraordinary and the most dangerous mob in Minecraft – even considered a malfunction. It has destroyed your world leaving you with nothing but a few parrots. How will you ever get your world back to its original state?

Complete the Comic

Base your comic on the story you just wrote.

TITLE:_____

Write Your Own Story

Base your story on the illustration.

Add an illustration.

Write a Creative Story Using this Word List

Use math to finish the picture and find out what your story should be about.

NOUNS:
vacuous
aberration
accessible
activator

aesthetics
ADJECTIVES:
punctilious
ramshackle
rife

terra-cotta
treacherous
VERBS:
build
create

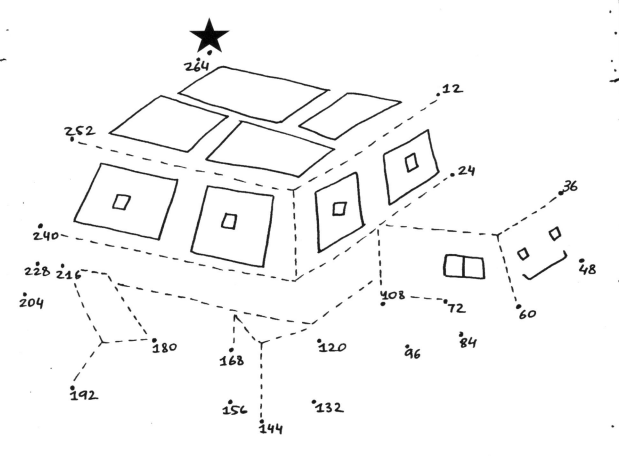

Connect the dots by skip counting by TWELVES.

_____
_____
_____
_____
_____
_____
_____
_____
_____
_____
_____
_____
_____
_____
_____
_____
_____
_____
_____

Vocabulary Building:

Define three words that are not familiar to you:

1. _____

2. _____

3. _____

Finish the Story

You are at a pillager outpost and your iron golem dies. The pillagers all point their crossbows at you, ready to fire. You see no way of escape so

Complete the Comic

Base your comic on the story you just wrote.

TITLE:_____

Write Your Own Story

Base your story on the illustration.

Add an illustration.

Write a Creative Story Using this Word List

Use math to finish the picture and find out what your story should be about.

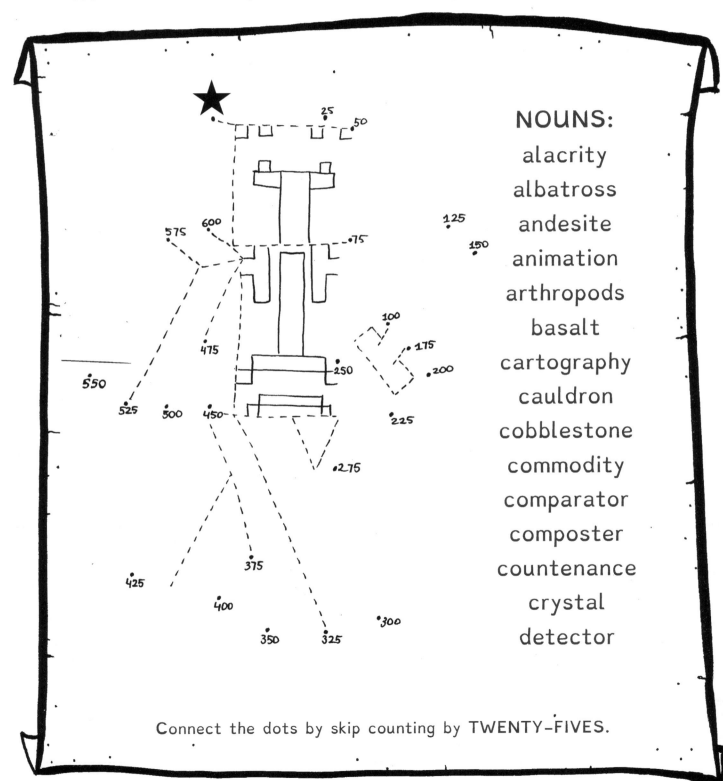

NOUNS:
alacrity
albatross
andesite
animation
arthropods
basalt
cartography
cauldron
cobblestone
commodity
comparator
composter
countenance
crystal
detector

Connect the dots by skip counting by TWENTY-FIVES.

_____
_____
_____
_____
_____
_____
_____
_____
_____
_____
_____
_____
_____
_____
_____
_____
_____
_____
_____

Vocabulary Building:

Define three words that are not familiar to you:

1. _____

2. _____

3. _____

Finish the Story

After some adventurous exploring, I was navigating my way back with my compass when I noticed a skeleton horse and rider.

Thunder and lightning struck and three more spawned with enchanted bows and chain armor. I needed to make a daring escape or defend myself, but I only had two diamonds, eight wood, one iron, and a

_____

_____

_____

_____

_____

_____

_____

_____

_____

_____

_____

_____

_____

_____

_____

_____

_____

_____

_____

_____

Complete the Comic

Base your comic on the story you just wrote.

TITLE:_____

Write Your Own Story

Base your story on the illustration.

Add an illustration.

Write a Creative Story Using this Word List

Use math to finish the picture and find out what your story should be about.

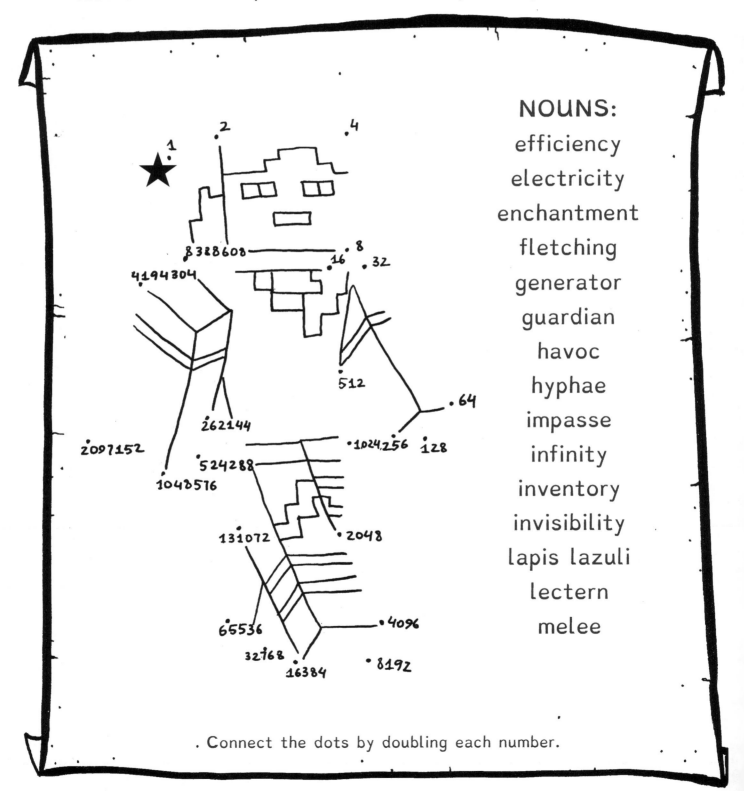

NOUNS:
efficiency
electricity
enchantment
fletching
generator
guardian
havoc
hyphae
impasse
infinity
inventory
invisibility
lapis lazuli
lectern
melee

Connect the dots by doubling each number.

Vocabulary Building:

Define three words that are not familiar to you:

1._____

_____

2._____

_____

3._____

_____

Finish the Story

I walked slowly into my fancy bedroom and saw that my golden oak bed was broken and my ender chest left open. To rebuild my bed, wool and wood must be harvested, so off I go. The light faded as I stepped outside, only to find

_____

_____

_____

_____

_____

_____

_____

_____

_____

_____

_____

_____

_____

_____

_____

Finish the Story

I run through the biomes filled with dandelions hoping to find something less terrifying than a chest full of treasure, surrounded by Piglins who fill me with terror. Suddenly I realize left my diamonds back with my ender

_____

_____

_____

_____

_____

_____

_____

_____

_____

_____

_____

_____

_____

_____

Finish the Story

She rowed her ramshackle boat across the treacherous ocean, exhausted from exploring a nearby tropical jungle. Noticing something unusual, she steered towards it, fueled by a new rush of adrenaline. In her haste, she failed to notice the gargantuan guardians swimming near

_____

_____

_____

_____

_____

_____

_____

_____

_____

_____

_____

_____

_____

_____

_____

Finish the Story

He stepped precariously over the cobblestone bridge, keeping a watchful eye on the dormant ghast in the distance. His clothes were highly flammable and he had foolishly left his armor behind. He had to be wary or it would wake, causing a

_____

_____

_____

_____

_____

_____

_____

_____

_____

_____

_____

_____

_____

_____

Made in the USA
Columbia, SC
28 May 2024

36241584R00050